W9-BWF-426

Whereas recognition of the inherent DIGNITY and of the EQUAL and inalienable rights of all members of the human family is the foundation of FREEDOM JUSTICE and PEACE in the world, Wherea disregard and contempt fo human RIGHTS have resulted in barbarous act which have outraged the conscience of mankind, and the adven of a world in which HUMAN BEINGS shall enjoy freedom of SPEEC and belief and freedom from fear and want has been proclaime as the highest ASPIRATION of the common people, Whereas it i essential, if man is not to be compelled to have recourse, as last resort, to rebellion against tyranny and oppression, tha human rights should be protected by the rule of law, Whereas it i ESSENTIAL to promote the develop ment of friendly relations betwee nations, Whereas the peoples of the Unite Nations have in the Charter reaffirmed their faith in fundamenta human rights, in the DIGNITY and WORTH of the huma person and in the equal rights of men and women an have determined to promote SOCIAL PROGRESS and bette standards of life in larger freedom, Wherea Member States have pledged themselves to achieve, i co-operation with the United Nations, the promotion o UNIVERSAL RESPECT for and obser vance of human rights and fundamenta freedoms, Whereas a common understandin of these rights and freedoms is of the greates importance for the full realization of this pledge,

Now, Therefore THE GENERAL ASSEMBLY proclaims THI UNIVERSAL DECLARATIO commo standard of a peo ples and all tha every individua or gan of society, ratio constantly in b TEACHING and romot respect for these d b progressive measure ation al, to secure their cogni tion and observance, Membe States themselves o territories under the

EVERY HUMAN HAS RIGHTS

EVERY HUMAN HAS RIGHTS

A PHOTOGRAPHIC DECLARATION FOR KIDS

BASED ON THE UNITED NATIONS
UNIVERSAL DECLARATION OF HUMAN RIGHTS

WITH POETRY FROM THE ePals COMMUNITY

FOREWORD BY MARY ROBINSON,
FORMER UNITED NATIONS HIGH COMMISSIONER FOR HUMAN RIGHTS

NATIONAL GEOGRAPHIC
WASHINGTON, D.C.

A NOTE FROM MARY ROBINSON

Former President of Ireland and former UN High Commissioner for Human Rights
Founder and President, Realizing Rights: The Ethical Globalization Initiative

WE ALL BELIEVE IN FREEDOM, but what exactly does "freedom" mean? Some say it is being able to decide by yourself what to do and how to do it. Others think it means having no rules at all. But human freedom means much more.

For me, Nelson Mandela summed it up best in his autobiography, *Long Walk to Freedom,* when referring to the struggles of South Africa to overcome apartheid, the system where people were treated differently based on their skin color:

> The truth is that we are not yet free; we have merely achieved the freedom to be free, the right not to be oppressed. We have not taken the final step of our journey, but the first step on a longer and even more difficult road. For to be free is not merely to cast off one's chains, but to live in a way that respects and enhances the freedom of others.

Sixty years ago, in the aftermath of World War II, the Holocaust, and the use of nuclear weapons, nations came together to forge a common understanding of the fundamental freedoms which were owed to all. The result was the Universal Declaration of Human Rights. It affirms the "inherent dignity" of all members of the human family. The Declaration spells out what human freedom is all about by proclaiming rights to freedom of opinion, expression, and belief and the right to a democratic government with fair laws that protect us all. But just as firmly and with equal emphasis, it proclaims the economic, social, and cultural rights—to food, to safe water, to health, to education, to shelter—to which we are all entitled. It also makes clear that all of these rights are to be enjoyed by all people without distinction of any kind.

The Universal Declaration ranks as one of the greatest documents of human history. I have spent much of my life working with others to ensure that governments live up to these commitments. In our rapidly globalizing world, it is especially important to make it clear to corporations, civil society organizations, and individuals that we all have responsibilities for making human rights a reality.

I wish I could say that we were on the verge of success, that the human rights celebrated in this book are protected for all people. But I can't. We still have widespread discrimination on the basis of gender, ethnicity, religious belief, or sexual orientation. Tragically, genocide—one group of people killing another because they are different—is happening again.

Poverty is continuing to trap millions of our fellow sisters and brothers in lives of despair.

FOREWORD

There are people dying for lack of water, food, or proper health care and people being killed for practicing (or not practicing) a religion, or for saying what they think about their government.

So what can we do? What role can each of us play in achieving true human freedom for all?

Change comes about through education. So it's important to know and understand what human rights are and what commitments our governments have made to realize those rights in practice. Reading this book is an excellent start down that road. The photographs and contributions by young people in these pages provide important lessons that can help you gain not just knowledge but emotional understanding of the rights that we all must defend.

Yet change doesn't come about just through knowledge—it also requires action. If you feel ready, the next step is to read the full text of the Universal Declaration included at the end of the book and then learn how you can work for human rights close to home and around the world.

To mark the 60th anniversary of the Universal Declaration, a diverse group of organizations have come together around the Elders' Every Human Has Rights Campaign. Our aim is to foster a global conversation on the values that unite us as one human family and put the power of human rights back in the hands of individuals and communities all over the world.

Go to the website EveryHumanHasRights.org to get involved. You can start by making your own pledge to live by the principles of the Universal Declaration. By doing so, you will be adding your voice to a growing global movement of people demanding that realizing the rights affirmed more than half a century ago becomes the priority for the 21st century.

EDITOR'S NOTE

EVERY HUMAN HAS RIGHTS is a collaboration among The Elders, National Geographic, and the ePals Global Community.

The Elders, a network of elder statesmen that advocates for human rights around the world, brought the 60th anniversary of the Universal Declaration of Human Rights to our attention and shared their Every Human Has Rights concept, their logo (showcased on the book as our title type), and their passion for human rights and the continued relevance of the Declaration. We are in awe of their work and decided to join their anniversary celebration by creating an interpretive book for young people.

Our starting point was kids themselves. We worked closely with ePals to develop a writing contest and invite the huge network of teachers and students that make up the ePals community to join the celebration. Each participating teacher shared the Universal Declaration, rewritten for accessibility, with his or her students. The students then wrote short responses and sent them to us for judging. What came from those thoughtful and sensitive young people moved all of us who worked on the book.

Then the National Geographic team got to work. Inspired by the Declaration, the Elders, and the work of the 16 contest winners, the team created the book design, found photos, and wrote captions and labels.

Mary Robinson, one of the Elders as well as former President of Ireland and former U.N. High Commissioner of Human Rights, agreed to write the foreword.

So now it is your turn. Read this book and pass it along. Talk about human rights with your friends and family. Go to www.EveryHumanHasRights.org and sign the Declaration. Speak up, participate in your government, respect yourself and others, and do everything you can to help realize the dream of human rights for everyone everywhere.

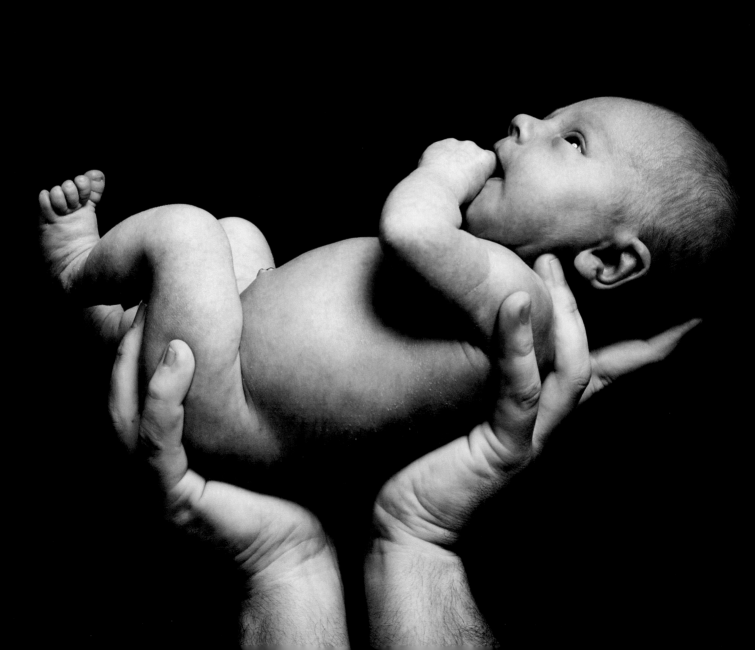

Listen, my children, listen to me
Each of you was born, crafted from earth
Bound to the land, sea, and sky
And from the moment you drew your first breath
You were free
Never to kneel before your brother
And call him master
For you were both crafted of the same earth

—Lauren Auer, age 18

All humans are born FREE with the same dignity and rights.

In Chiapas, Mexico, native women—like other women around the world—have organized to let their leaders know that their rights and dignity should be respected.

DIGNITY

Just as this two-week-old baby needs the protection of its parents, all humans need the protection of their governments in order to thrive.

Some people see only skin deep, but there is so much more to a person than the color of their skin. Why would you hurt me just because I'm different? Just because I don't look like you? Nobody has the right to mistreat me just because I don't look, think, or act like you. When will this world learn that everyone was created equal? If everyone looks, thinks, and acts exactly the same? Imagine what a world that would be. But all I'm asking for is that you show me some respect, even if you don't think I deserve it.

—Kathryn Buonantony, age 13

When young people, like this American teenager, see no hope of being protected and respected by their society, they may join street gangs and use violence to force people to respect them.

The right to worship or not worship as you choose is protected in numerous countries. From left to right, these pictures show a Balinese Hindu in Indonesia; Christian children in the U.S.; and a Muslim woman in Dakar, Senegal.

Everyone has the same rights.

It doesn't matter what **GENDER** you are.

It doesn't matter what **COLOR** your skin is,

what **LANGUAGE** you speak,

what **RELIGION** you practice,

how **RICH** or **POOR** you are,

how **DIFFERENT** you are from those around you,

or what country you come from.

It doesn't even matter whether your own government agrees with these rights.

Your rights are in **YOU** no matter what.

Laughing is what you do when something is funny.
Ice cream is what you eat—it's sweet as honey.
Fun is what you call it when you play.
Equality is what you have every single day.
There it is, right in your face.
You have a life to live, so give it space!

—Nakayla Griffin, age 11

Boys return to their village near Usuru, Tanzania, at the end
of the day. Like many countries, Tanzania has a mixed record
on human rights. It honors some, like freedom of speech, but
not others, such as equal rights for women.

You have the right to a free and safe **LIFE.**

Kids play in the streets of Havana, Cuba, where everyone has the right to free education and free health care, but elections aren't free and fair.

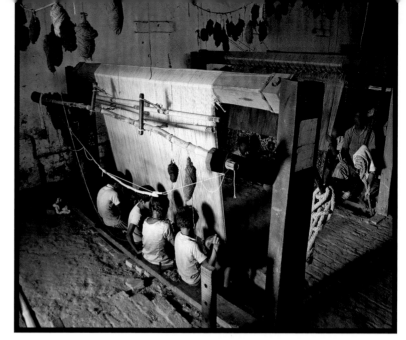

These children are at work in a carpet factory in India. Though slavery is illegal throughout the world, some companies continue to use enslaved people, stolen or bought from their families, as workers.

Nobody has the right to make you a **SLAVE.**

Unheard Words

I have rights, and I have wishes.
We all have rights, and we all have wishes.
I have the right to be free, we all do.
Slaves were never asked if they wanted to work,
Shedding tears and crying unheard words, in
Unbearable conditions and misery.
Collectively we can stop this evil.
So Why Does Slavery Still Exist?

—Tegen Dunnill Jones, age 13

A girl picks cotton in the Chira River Valley in Peru. Very poor families around the world need their children to work to help put food on the table. Human rights organizations are trying to improve economic conditions and eliminate child labor so children can go to school. Educated kids grow into adults more likely to break the cycle of poverty.

FREEDOM

Asylum.
Safety.
I, too, need protection.
If I don't feel secure,
I toss and turn in fear.
I can't continue.

—Mei Huan Lafferty-Levdansky, age 11

Violence against women is common in the United States—where this woman lives—as well as around the world. The U.S. is one of 165 countries that have passed laws that make domestic violence illegal.

Nobody has the right to **TORTURE** you, **BULLY** you,

or punish you too severely.

SAFETY

Every human in the world must be treated as a **PERSON**.

The Universal Declaration of Human Rights was inspired by the terrible genocide and dehumanization that occurred during the Holocaust. These prisoners in a concentration camp in Austria were starved and forced to be guinea pigs in scientific experiments.

Trapped

Within the dark walls, we are all trapped.
The walls are not brick, nor wood, nor metal
The walls around us are hate
There is no other ingredient to the mixture they spread,
As the walls become higher around us
There is no escaping, even when the walls are gone
The hate contained will remain within us all
Trapped within the walls

—Tayler Oakes, age 14

7

Everyone has the right to be treated **EQUALLY** before the law.

JUSTICE

Under a just legal system, neither money nor power nor influence should affect fair treatment.

All over the world, unfair arrests break up families.

A Backyard that Once Was

"Put your hands up!" the soldier yells.

"Momma! Why are you leaving? Take me with you! I need you!"

"Back away!" the soldier orders.

There, in our backyard that once was, I watch you leave.

I see you go and one tear wanders down your face meaning, "Goodbye."

I cry for you and long for you, knowing life will never be the same.

Years go by; I will be much older.

But I will wait for you in the backyard that once was.

—Sara Sachs, age 12

If your rights aren't **RESPECTED,** you should be able to get help from the law.

NOBODY has the right to arrest you or put you in prison unfairly.

PROTECTION

If you are accused of a crime, you have the right to a **FAIR** trial.

DD

You are **INNOCENT** until proven guilty.

An Israeli soldier talks with a Palestinian family after an arrest in 1988. People arrested by a government that is not their own have the same rights to the protection of the law as do citizens of that country.

You have the right to **PRIVACY.**

Nobody can tell lies about you, and nobody can look at your

private belongings, writings,

or body without your **PERMISSION.**

In some but not all countries, the law guarantees women and children rights over their own bodies.

PRIVACY

I hold my diary very dear. If anyone were to look in it, I'd say, Human rights are real, and if you don't respect them or me, you may walk away with your head down in shame.

—Moon Nickola, age 10

In Nice, France, in 2005, a city employee monitors street cameras placed around the city. With fear of terrorism rampant, governments around the world struggle to balance privacy rights with security concerns.

MOVEMENT

13

You have the right to **MOVE** around within your country.

You have the right to **LEAVE** your country

and **COME BACK** to it if and when you want to.

        Safety
Running excitedly with my friends
playing in my bedroom
Swimming by myself

        Danger
But in Ethiopia I was in the dark
all alone with someone trying to kill me.
I walked fast with fear.
I was scared, but no more.

—Nyakuma War, age 16

If you aren't **SAFE** in your country, you have the right

to go to another country.

A family displaced by war walks across the border from Ethiopia to Eritrea.

People all over the world are proud of their countries. From left to right, kids with a Brazilian flag at a soccer match in Venezuela, a Jamaican flag in England, an American flag in the U.S., and Singapore flags in Singapore.

My mother is Indian, my dad Mauritanian. I was born in England. But we all live in America where my little brother was born. My best friend is half Hispanic and half German, and she was born in America, too. I am thankful for this human right because I might not have found my good friends or have this happy life without it.

—Anjali Nemorin, age 11

You have the right

to **BELONG** to a country.

NATIONALITY

MARRIAGE

A family with their marriage license in California in 2008, soon after that U.S. state legalized same-sex marriage. Six countries—Canada, the United Kingdom, the Netherlands, Belgium, Spain, and South Africa—have extended marriage rights to same-sex couples.

Mandla Mandela, grandson of former South African President Nelson Mandela, and his bride Tando Mabunu, dance at their traditional Xhosa wedding in South Africa.

Every adult has the right to **MARRY** and have a family,

but nobody can **FORCE** you to get married.

In marriage, both partners are **EQUAL.**

17

You have the **RIGHT** to your **OWN THINGS.**

A Mongolian nomad woman in front of her yurt, a house that can be taken apart and moved when needed. Mongolia's constitution guarantees women equal rights, including the right to own property.

We are free to do anything we wish. No one can tell us what to do or how to to it. We can swim in a canal or kayak in a lake, meet our friends at the movies and see anything we like. We are free to make our own choices. We have the right to create what we want, even sing a song about God. We have real freedom!

—Sarah Kitzmann, age 12

You have the right to **BELIEVE** anything you want, to practice or not practice your **FAITH,** and to change your beliefs at any time.

19

You have the right to have any opinion and to **CREATE** art of any kind.

You have the right to **SHARE** your opinions and your art

with anyone from any country.

Holding torches, about 3,500 people in Budapest, Hungary, assemble peacefully to form a peace sign during a 2006 rally against the war in Iraq.

ASSEMBLY

20

You have the right to **MEET** with others

PEACEFULLY for any purpose, but no one can force you to join a

group if you don't want to.

An Equal Say

A right to an equal say
Is guaranteed in the USA
From Atlantic to Pacific,
From the Great Lakes to Santa Fe.
Everywhere you go,
No need to lie low,
When the time is right,
It's your turn to put on a show.
Topping it all,
Whether Spring or Fall,
Never forget,
An equal say is for all.

—John Xuecheng Fan, age 12

In 2004, former U.S. President Jimmy Carter (in tan plaid shirt) and former Thai Prime Minister Chuan Leekpai (standing next to Carter) observe Indonesia's first direct presidential election to make sure it is free and fair.

Every adult has the right to an equal say in the government

and an equal opportunity to work for the government.

Every country must hold free and fair **ELECTIONS**.

Candidate for Parliament Safia Siddiqi votes on October 9, 2004, in the first free and fair elections in Afghanistan since 1969.

DEMOCRACY

I see children and adults roaming the streets and not having anywhere to go. It is just sickening. I think these people deserve a break and to have a decent life. They didn't do anything, so why should they suffer? People say many have died and, "I don't know them, why should I help them?" Well, they're wrong. Just by doing one little thing, they can change people's lives, and that could start something. These people have a right to a decent life, so let them have it.

—Caleb Pruzinsky, age 13

This child is one of over 10,000 homeless people who live on the streets in the downtown area of São Paulo, Brazil.

You have the right to get **HELP** from your government

if you are out of work, sick, disabled, old, or can't **MAKE**

enough money to **LIVE** on for any other reason.

SOCIAL SECURITY

A construction worker in Chennai, India

An electronics equipment assembly line in Hong Kong, China

A hairdresser in Onicha, Nigeria

All adults have the right to **WORK** and must be paid for

their work and treated fairly and equally in the workplace.

You have the right to

FREE time.

WORK and LEISURE

After a long day at school, many kids—like these in the U.S.—have a chance to relax in play.

25

You have the right to **FOOD, SHELTER,** and **HEALTH CARE.**

Compassionate people and organizations help people around the world. Left, a soup kitchen set up for the holy month of Ramadan in the Balata refugee camp in Palestine. Center, two agencies—one from the U.S. and one from Haiti—work together to build homes for impoverished Haitians. Right, a health worker (in white) in a refugee camp in Chad cares for a refugee from the Darfur region of Sudan.

Reading, writing, and arithmetic
I'm just hoping it will all stick
It's my right to learn and obtain an education
When I'm done, I'll go on vacation

—Sydney Schmit, age 11

You have the right to go to **SCHOOL** for free.

27

You have the right to enjoy culture, **ARTS,**

and scientific progress. You have the right to own

anything you create or discover.

PARTICIPATION

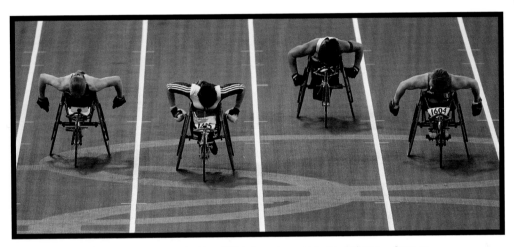

The women's 100-meter race at the 2004 Paralympics in Athens, Greece. International sporting events for disabled people showcase their abilities and encourage societies to make every aspect of culture accessible to all.

PEACE

28

You have the right to **LIVE** in a world

where **EVERYONE'S** human rights are respected.

Tanzania started free public schools in 2001. There are not enough teachers yet, so some classes have as many as 140 students.

Two Kids, Two Beliefs

Holding a black, vast firearm

When you could be holding up two fingers for peace

Like the kid next to you.

He is peace. He is freedom.

You aren't either of those.

I know what my choice is. Choose yours.

Two kids.

Two beliefs.

—Rebecca Hayden, age 12

Speaking out against violence in your community is one way to help further the cause of human rights.

You must take responsibility for PROTECTING your own RIGHTS and the rights of others.

In 1988, Germany united under a democratic government and thousands of Germans gathered to tear down the Berlin Wall, which had separated communist East Berlin and democratic West Berlin.

RESPONSIBILITY

After 33 years of human rights abuses by a minority white government, South Africans—including these soccer players—are working toward a future in which everyone's rights are respected.

Is freedom something that's so sweet?
Is it a word that makes your mother
Cry with joy or makes your father get on his knees
And say what Martin Luther King said:
Free at last! Free at last! Thank God Almighty
We're free at last!

—Maya Copeland, age 12

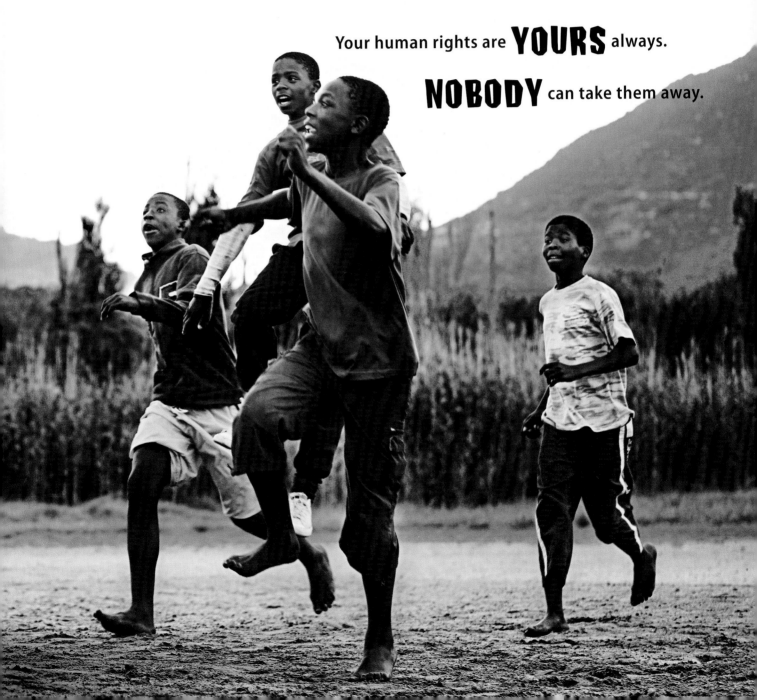

Your human rights are **YOURS** always.

NOBODY can take them away.

UNIVERSAL DECLARATION OF HUMAN RIGHTS

Adopted by UN General Assembly Resolution 217A (III) of 10 December 1948

WHEREAS recognition of the inherent dignity and of the equal and inalienable rights of all members of the human family is the foundation of freedom, justice and peace in the world,

WHEREAS disregard and contempt for human rights have resulted in barbarous acts which have outraged the conscience of mankind, and the advent of a world in which human beings shall enjoy freedom of speech and belief and freedom from fear and want has been proclaimed as the highest aspiration of the common people,

WHEREAS it is essential, if man is not to be compelled to have recourse, as a last resort, to rebellion against tyranny and oppression, that human rights should be protected by the rule of law,

WHEREAS it is essential to promote the development of friendly relations between nations,

WHEREAS the peoples of the United Nations have in the Charter reaffirmed their faith in fundamental human rights, in the dignity and worth of the human person and in the equal rights of men and women and have determined to promote social progress and better standards of life in larger freedom,

WHEREAS Member States have pledged themselves to achieve, in cooperation with the United Nations, the promotion of universal respect for and observance of human rights and fundamental freedoms,

WHEREAS a common understanding of these rights and freedoms is of the greatest importance for the full realization of this pledge,

Now, therefore, *The General Assembly* Proclaims

THIS UNIVERSAL DECLARATION OF HUMAN RIGHTS as a common standard of achievement for all peoples and all nations, to the end that every individual and every organ of society, keeping this Declaration constantly in mind, shall strive by teaching and education to promote respect for these rights and freedoms and by progressive measures, national and international, to secure their universal and effective recognition and observance, both among the peoples of Member States themselves and among the peoples of territories under their jurisdiction.

1 All human beings are born free and equal in dignity and rights. They are endowed with reason and conscience and should act towards one another in a spirit of brotherhood.

2 Furthermore, no distinction shall be made on the basis of the political, jurisdictional or international status of the country or territory to which a person belongs, whether it be independent, trust, non-self-governing or under any other limitation of sovereignty.

3 Everyone has the right to life, liberty and security of person.

4 No one shall be held in slavery or servitude; slavery and the slave trade shall be prohibited in all their forms.

5 No one shall be subjected to torture or to cruel, inhuman or degrading treatment or punishment.

6 Everyone has the right to recognition everywhere as a person before the law.

7 All are equal before the law and are entitled without any discrimination to equal protection of the law. All are entitled to equal protection against any discrimination in violation of the Declaration and against any incitement to such discrimination.

8 Everyone has the right to an effective remedy by the competent national tribunals for acts violating the fundamental rights granted him by the constitution or by law.

9 No one shall be subjected to arbitrary arrest, detention or exile.

10 Everyone is entitled in full equality to a fair and public hearing by an independent and impartial tribunal, in the determination of his rights and obligations and of any criminal charge against him.

11 1 Everyone charged with a penal offense has the right to be presumed innocent until proved guilty according to law in a public trial at which he has had all the guarantees necessary for his defense.

2 No one shall be held guilty of any penal offense on account of any act or omission which did not constitute a penal offense, under national or international law, at the time it was committed. Nor shall a heavier penalty be imposed than the one that was applicable at the time the penal offense was committed.

12 No one shall be subjected to arbitrary interference with his privacy, family, home or correspondence, nor to attacks upon his honor and reputation. Everyone has the right to the protection of the law against such interference or attacks.

13 1 Everyone has the right to freedom of movement and residence within the borders of each state.

2 Everyone has the right to leave any country, including his own, and to return to his country.

14 1 Everyone has the right to seek and to enjoy in other countries asylum from persecution.

2 This right may not be invoked in the case of prosecutions genuinely arising from non-political crimes or from acts contrary to the purposes and principles of the United Nations.

15 1 Everyone has the right to a nationality.

2 No one shall be arbitrarily deprived of his nationality nor denied the right to change his nationality.

Former First Lady Eleanor Roosevelt chaired the U.N. committee that wrote the Declaration.

You can find this document at http://www.un.org/cyberschoolbus/humanrights/resources/universal.asp.
You can also check out the plain language version at http://www.un.org/cyberschoolbus/humanrights/resources/plain.asp

16 1 Men and women of full age, without any limitation due to race, nationality or religion, have the right to marry and to found a family. They are entitled to equal rights as to marriage, during marriage and at its dissolution.

2 Marriage shall be entered into only with the free and full consent of the intending spouses.

3 The family is the natural and fundamental group unit of society and is entitled to protection by society and the State.

17 1 Everyone has the right to own property alone as well as in association with others.

2 No one shall be arbitrarily deprived of his property.

18 Everyone has the right to freedom of thought, conscience and religion; this right includes freedom to change his religion or belief, and freedom, either alone or in community with others and in public or private, to manifest his religion or belief in teaching, practice, worship and observance.

19 Everyone has the right to freedom of opinion and expression: this right includes freedom to hold opinions without interference and to seek, receive and impart information and ideas through any media and regardless of frontiers.

20 1 Everyone has the right to freedom of peaceful assembly and association.

2 No one may be compelled to belong to an association.

21 1 Everyone has the right to take part in the government of his country, directly or through freely chosen representatives.

2 Everyone has the right of equal access to public service in his country.

3 The will of the people shall be the basis of the authority of government; this will shall be expressed in periodic and genuine elections which shall be by universal and equal suffrage and shall be held by secret vote or by equivalent free voting procedures.

22 Everyone, as a member of society, has the right to social security and is entitled to realization, through national effort and international co- operation and in accordance with the organization and resources of each State, of the economic, social and cultural rights indispensable for his dignity and the free development of his personality.

23 1 Everyone has the right to work, to free choice of employment, to just and favorable conditions of work and to protection against unemployment.

2 Everyone, without any discrimination, has the right to equal pay for equal work.

3 Everyone who works has the right to just and favorable remuneration ensuring for himself and his family an existence worthy of human dignity, and supplemented, if necessary, by other means of social protection.

4 Everyone has the right to form and to join trade unions for the protection of his interests.

24 Everyone has the right to rest and leisure, including reasonable limitation of working hours and periodic holidays with pay.

25 1 Everyone has the right to a standard of living adequate for the health and well-being of himself and of his family, including food, clothing, housing and medical care and necessary social services, and the right to security in the event of unemployment, sickness, disability, widowhood, old age or other lack of livelihood in circumstances beyond his control.

2 Motherhood and childhood are entitled to special care and assistance. All children, whether born in or out of wedlock, shall enjoy the same social protection.

26 1 Everyone has the right to education. Education shall be free, at least in the elementary and fundamental stages. Elementary education shall be compulsory. Technical and professional education shall be made generally available and higher education shall be equally accessible to all on the basis of merit.

2 Education shall be directed to the full development of the human personality and to the strengthening of respect for human rights and fundamental freedoms. It shall promote understanding, tolerance and friendship among all nations, racial or religious groups, and shall further the activities of the United Nations for the maintenance of peace.

3 Parents have a prior right to choose the kind of education that shall be given to their children.

27 1 Everyone has the right freely to participate in the cultural life of the community, to enjoy the arts and to share in scientific advancement and its benefits.

2 Everyone has the right to the protection of the moral and material interests resulting from any scientific, literary or artistic production of which he is the author.

28 Everyone is entitled to a social and international order in which the rights and freedoms set forth in this Declaration can be fully realized.

29 1 Everyone has duties to the community in which alone the free and full development of his personality is possible.

2 In the exercise of his rights and freedoms, everyone shall be subject only to such limitations as are determined by law solely for the purpose of securing due recognition and respect for the rights and freedoms of others and of meeting the just requirements of morality, public order and the general welfare in a democratic society.

3 These rights and freedoms may in no case be exercised contrary to the purposes and principles of the United Nations.

30 Nothing in this Declaration may be interpreted as implying for any State, group or person any right to engage in any activity or to perform any act aimed at the destruction of any of the rights and freedoms set forth herein.

Mary Robinson

The first woman President of Ireland (1990-1997) and more recently United Nations High Commissioner for Human Rights (1997-2002), Mary Robinson has been a human rights advocate for most of her life. She is currently founder and president of Realizing Rights: The Ethical Globalization Initiative and one of the Elders, a group of elder statesmen working for human rights around the world. As a professor, legislator, and lawyer, Mary Robinson has always sought to use law as an instrument for social change, arguing landmark cases before the European Court of Human Rights as well as in the Irish courts and the European Court in Luxembourg.

The recipient of numerous honors and awards throughout the world, Mary Robinson is Chair of the Council of Women World Leaders and Vice President of the Club of Madrid. She chairs the International Board of the International Institute for Environment and Development (IIED) and the Fund for Global Human Rights, and is Honorary President of Oxfam International and Patron of the International Community of Women Living with AIDS (ICW). She serves on several boards, including the Vaccine Fund and the Global Compact, is a member of the Royal Irish Academy and the American Philosophical Society, and chairs the Irish Chamber Orchestra.

The National Geographic and ePals Human Rights Writing Contest Winners:

Lauren Auer is a freshman pre-med student at the University of Southern Mississippi and is passionate about horses and writing. She wrote this poem in Charlotte Griffin's class at W. P. Davidson School in Mobile, Alabama.

Kathryn Buonantony is a student at Flood Middle School in Stratford, Connecticut. She likes singing, acting, writing, laughing, hanging out with her friends and family, playing with her dog Grace, baseball, listening to music, and playing basketball. Her favorite subject is art. She wrote her piece in Mrs. Kaluzynski's class.

Nakayla Griffin is a student at Team Academy in Newark, New Jersey. Reading and writing are her favorite subjects, but she also finds time for the cheerleading squad. She wrote her poem in Miss Nagel's class.

Tegen Dunnill Jones is from Calgary, Canada. She is home schooled by her mom, and her hobbies include swimming, biking, and hanging out with friends. She aspires to be a vet and teacher in Africa.

Mei Huan Lafferty-Levdansky's favorite school subjects are art, math, science, social studies, and creative writing. She enjoys sports, especially soccer and softball. She plans on going to college and becoming an actress. Mei Huan wrote her poem in Sara Levine's class at Maplewood-Richmond Heights School in St. Louis, Missouri.

Tayler Oakes is a quiet girl who loves to read and write. She's really close to her friends and wants to become a writer or clothing designer. She wrote her poem in Miss Kettler's class at Granite Falls Middle School in Granite Falls, Washington.

Sara Sachs has been dancing competitively for 9 years, plays the violin, and loves to read. She hopes to be a cultural anthropologist when she grows up. She wrote her poem in Kristin Sanchez's class at Newtown Friends School in Newtown, Pennsylvania

Moon Nickola lives with her parents, two brothers, one sister, and two cats in Grand Blanc, Michigan, where she enjoys dance classes, playing tennis, and jumping on her trampoline. Moon is a fifth grader at Grand Blanc City School and thinks about being a hairdresser because she has had lots of practice on her dolls, or maybe a poet. She wrote her poem in Vicki Weiss's class.

Nyakuma War was born in Ethiopia. Her family moved to Sudan, then to Egypt, and finally to Ballarat, Victoria, Australia, to avoid wars going on around them. She likes basketball and dancing and plans to be a dancer when she grows up. Nyakuma wrote her poem in Sofia Thapa's class at Ballarat Secondary School.

Anjali Nemorin loves to read, write, play the piano, and bake. She wrote her piece in Mrs. Gayle Richardson's class at Lawton Elementary School in Ann Arbor, Michigan.

Sarah Kitzmann likes to read, draw, and write stories. She is home schooled by her mother in Rock Hill, South Carolina.

John Xuecheng Fan is a seventh grader in Ann Arbor, Michigan. His hobbies include writing, reading, fishing, taking pictures, and swimming. He plays piano and percussion and totally loves sharks! When he grows up, he plans to be a doctor or a marine biologist. He wrote his poem in Mrs. Gayle Richardson's class at Lawton Elementary School.

Caleb Pruzinsky is from Stratford, Connecticut. He likes to skateboard, play the drums, ride quads, play baseball and football, and hang out with friends. He is an eighth grader at Flood Middle School. He wrote his piece in Sarah Kaluzynski's class.

Sydney Schmit swims on a competition swim team, loves to write, and wants to be an Olympic swimmer or a model. She wrote her poem in Mrs. Vicki Weiss's class at Grand Blanc City School, in Grand Blanc, Michigan.

Rebecca Hayden enjoys soccer and basketball and loves to read. She wrote her poem in Kristin Sanchez's class at Newtown Friends School in Newtown, Pennsylvania.

Maya Copeland lives in White Plains, New York.

About ePals:

The ePals Global Learning Community™ (www.epals.com) is the largest online community of K-12 learners, enabling more than half a million educators and their students across 200 countries and territories to safely connect, exchange ideas, and work together. The company's mission is to support lifelong learning through collaborative experiences that empower and inspire. ePals is especially committed to supporting the right to education by enabling academically rigorous educational opportunities in economically disadvantaged environments worldwide through the ePals Foundation—provider of In2Books, the company's flagship literacy eMentoring program.

Further information

To find out more, check out these websites. Please note that reports of human rights abuses can be very disturbing and may not be appropriate for children under 12. Sights safe for younger children are marked with an asterisk.

*Every Human Has Rights
www.everyhumanhasrights.org
Go there to sign the Universal Declaration of Human Rights.

Amnesty International
www.amnesty.org
Amnesty International is a worldwide movement of people who campaign for internationally recognized human rights to be respected and protected for everyone.

Global Call to Action Against Poverty
www.whiteband.org/Action/take-action/take-action-stop-the-food-crisis/
GCAP is the world's largest civil society movement calling for an end to poverty and inequality.

Human Rights Watch
www.hrw.org/
Human Rights Watch works to prevent discrimination, to uphold political freedom, to protect people from inhumane conduct in wartime, and to bring offenders to justice.

Internews
www.internews.org/
Internews works to harness the power of media and information to help people hold their governments accountable, develop tolerant and prosperous communities, and to make sense of the driving forces affecting their lives.

Save the Children
www.savethechildren.org.uk/
Save the Children is the world's largest independent organization advocating for the rights of children.

Unicef
www.unicef.org/
UNICEF, and agency of the United Nations, works in over 150 countries and territories to supports child health and nutrition, good water and sanitation, quality basic education for all boys and girls, and the protection of children from violence, exploitation, and AIDS.

United Nations Know Your Rights
www.knowyourrights2008.org/index.
php?nave=home
On this site, the United Nations celebrates the 60th anniversary of the Universal Declaration of Human Rights.

*United Nations Universal Declaration of Human Rights 60th Anniversary Youth Center
www.un.org/events/humanrights/udhr60/youth.shtml
Anniversary information and activities especially for young people.

United States Department of State Bureau of Democracy, Human Rights, and Labor 2007 Country Reports on Human Rights Practices
www.state.gov/g/drl/rls/hrrpt/2007/
The United States government site reporting on human rights abuses outside the U.S.

University of Minnesota Human Rights Library
www1.umn.edu/humanrts/about.html
A collection of more than 85,000 core human rights documents, including human rights treaties and other primary international human rights instruments. The site also provides access to more than 4,000 links and a search device for multiple human rights sites.

Witness
hub.witness.org (no www)
An online forum where individuals, organizations, networks, and groups around the world bring their human rights stories and campaigns to global attention.

Library of Congress Cataloging-in-Publication Data
available upon request.
Hardcover ISBN: 978-1-4263-0510-8
Library ISBN: 978-1-4263-0511-5

PUBLISHED BY THE NATIONAL GEOGRAPHIC SOCIETY
John M. Fahey, Jr., President and Chief Executive Officer
Gilbert M. Grosvenor, Chairman of the Board
Tim T. Kelly, President, Global Media Group
John Q. Griffin, President, Publishing
Nina D. Hoffman, Executive Vice President; President,
    Book Publishing Group

PREPARED BY THE BOOK DIVISION
Nancy Laties Feresten, Vice President, Editor in Chief,
    Children's Books
Bea Jackson, Director of Design and Illustrations,
    Children's Books
Amy Shields, Executive Editor, Series, Children's Books
Jennifer Emmett, Executive Editor, Reference and
    Solo, Children's Books
Carl Mehler, Director of Maps

STAFF FOR THIS BOOK
Nancy Laties Feresten, Editor
Bea Jackson, Art Director
Lori Epstein, Illustrations Editor
Bea Jackson, Jim Hiscott, David M. Seager, Designers
Jennifer Eaton, Editorial Intern
Rahel Tesfahun, Editorial Intern
Jennifer A. Thornton, Managing Editor
Grace Hill, Associate Managing Editor
R. Gary Colbert, Production Director
Lewis Bassford, Production Manager
Susan Borke, Legal and Business Affairs

MANUFACTURING AND QUALITY MANAGEMENT
Christopher A. Liedel, Chief Financial Officer
Phillip L. Schlosser, Vice President
Chris Brown, Technical Director
Nicole Elliott, Rachel Faulise, Monika Lynde, Managers

Founded in 1888, the National Geographic society is one of the largest scientific and educational organizations in the world. It reaches more than 285 million people worldwideeach month through its official journal, NATIONAL GEOGRAPHIC, and its four other magazines; The National Geographic Channel; television documentaries; radio programs; films; books; videos and DVDs; maps; and interactive media. National Geographic has funded more than 8,000 scientific research projects and supports an education program combating geographic illiteracy.

For more information please call 1-800-NGS-LINE (647-5463). Or write to the following address:

NATIONAL GEOGRAPHIC SOCIETY
1145 17th Street N.W.
Washington, D.C. 20036-4688 U.S.A.
Visit the Society's Web site:
www.nationalgeographic.com/books

Printed in Canada

Visit us online at: www.nationalgeographic.com/books
For librarians and teachers: www.ngchildrensbooks.com
More for kids from National Geographic: kids.nationalgeographic.com
For information about special discounts for bulk purchases, please contact National Geographic Books Special Sales: ngspecsales@ngs.org
For rights or permissions inquiries, please contact National Geographic Books Subsidiary Rights: ngbookrights@ngs.org